LIBRA:

A COMPLETE GUIDE TO THE LIBRA ASTROLOGY STAR SIGN

Sofia Visconti

© **Copyright 2024 - All rights reserved.**

The content contained within this book may not be reproduced, duplicated or transmitted without direct written permission from the author or the publisher.

Under no circumstances will any blame or legal responsibility be held against the publisher, or author, for any damages, reparation, or monetary loss due to the information contained within this book, either directly or indirectly.

Legal Notice:

This book is copyright protected. It is only for personal use. You cannot amend, distribute, sell, use, quote or paraphrase any part, or the content within this book, without the consent of the author or publisher.

Disclaimer Notice:

Please note the information contained within this document is for educational and entertainment purposes only. All effort has been executed to present accurate, up to date, reliable, complete information. No warranties of any kind are declared or implied. Readers acknowledge that the author is not engaged in the rendering of legal, financial, medical or professional advice. The content within this book has been derived from various sources. Please consult a licensed professional before attempting any techniques outlined in this book.

By reading this document, the reader agrees that under no circumstances is the author responsible for any losses, direct or indirect, that are incurred as a result of the use of the information contained within this document, including, but not limited to, errors, omissions, or inaccuracies.

Subscribe To Sofia Visconti

As a subscriber you will receive a _Free Gift_ + You wil be the first to hear about new books, articles and more exclusives **just for you**

Click Here

Or Visit Below:
https://www.subscribepage.com/svmyth

Or Simply Scan The Qr Code To Join

Contents

INTRODUCTION 6
Libra Zodiac Sign Overview 8

CHAPTER 1: HISTORY AND MYTHOLOGY 12
Historical Origins of the Libra Constellation 12
Historical Events Under the Libra Season 15

CHAPTER 2: LOVE & COMPATIBILITY 19
The Libra Love approach 20
Compatibility with Other Zodiac Signs 22
Tips for Dating and Maintaining Relationships
with Libra 26

CHAPTER 3: FRIENDS AND FAMILY 29
Libra as a Friend 30
Libra and Family Dynamics 32
Challenges in Friendships and Family Relations
for Libra 34

CHAPTER 4: CAREER AND MONEY 38
Career Preferences and Professional Aspirations 39
Strengths in the Workplace 41
Challenges Faced by Libra and Strategies to
Overcome Them 43

CHAPTER 5: SELF-IMPROVEMENT 48
Personal Growth and Development 49
Harnessing Libra Strengths and Overcoming Weaknesses 51

CHAPTER 6: THE YEAR AHEAD 56
Horoscope Guide 57
Key Astrological Events and Their Impact on Libra 59
Key Life Areas 61

CHAPTER 7: FAMOUS LIBRA PERSONALITIES 66
Mahatma Gandhi 67
Serena Williams 68
John Lennon 68
Brigitte Bardot 69
Eminem 69
Margaret Thatcher 70
Dwight D. Eisenhower 70
Elisabeth Shue 71
Cardi B 72
Vladimir Putin 72
Alfred Nobel 73
Barbara Walters 74

CONCLUSION 76

INTRODUCTION

Welcome to the captivating world of astrology, where the movements of entities hold significance for our lives on Earth. At its core, astrology is an intricate belief system. One that examines the relationship between the positions and motions of bodies like planets and stars and their impact on human existence and personality traits. It is a field with roots that trace back thousands of years, across cultures worldwide.

Astrology operates under the principle that the positions of objects at the time of an individual's birth can provide insights into their character, behaviors and potential life paths. The positions of these bodies within the twelve zodiac signs form unique cosmic blueprints for each person known as birth charts. Astrologers interpret these charts to offer guidance, self awareness and a deeper understanding of oneself as well as their interactions with others.

In this book we embark on a journey to explore one of the signs of astrology. The Libra zodiac sign. The main objective of this book is to shed light on the mysterious Libra zodiac sign. If you happen to be a Libra or have someone close to you who is, then this book can serve as your window into unraveling the enigmatic traits of this air sign.

Our journey into Libra's world will include:

- **Understanding Libra:** We will explore the core traits, strengths and weaknesses of Libra individuals. Overall you will gain a comprehensive understanding of their unique character.
- **Love and Relationships**: Libras are renowned for their romantic and partnership-oriented nature. We will delve into how Libras approach love and relationships. Furthermore we will explore their compatibility with other zodiac signs.
- **Career and Ambitions**: Libras have a knack for diplomacy and collaboration. We will explore how these traits influence their career choices, work style and professional success.
- **Self-Discovery**: This book will serve as a tool for Libras and anyone interested in astrology to embark on a journey of self-discovery. We'll provide insights into personal growth and

harnessing Libra's innate qualities for personal development.
- **Astrological Guidance**: You'll find guidance on harnessing Libra's strengths, managing challenges and aligning with the cosmic energies to lead a fulfilling life.

Throughout this book, we'll draw on the wisdom of astrology, drawing connections between the celestial world and your personal experiences. Whether you're a Libra seeking to deepen your self-awareness or simply curious about astrology and its influence on your life. This promises to be an enlightening journey into the world of astrology and the captivating Libra star sign.

LIBRA ZODIAC SIGN OVERVIEW

- **Date of Star Sign**: Libra falls between September 23rd and October 22nd, making it the seventh sign of the zodiac.
- **Symbol**: The symbol of Libra is the Scales, representing balance, harmony and justice. The scales are an emblem of the Libra's quest for equilibrium and fairness in all aspects of life.
- **Element**: Libra belongs to the Air element, along with Gemini and Aquarius. Air signs are associated with intellect, communication and social interaction. Libras are skilled at using their mental faculties to navigate the complexities of relationships and society.
- **Planet**: Venus, the planet of love and beauty, is the ruling planet of Libra. Venus brings a sense of

refinement, charm and aesthetic appreciation to Libra's personality and pursuits.
- **Color**: Libra's primary color is typically considered to be blue. Particularly shades that evoke peace and tranquility. Blue reflects their desire for balance and serenity in life.
- **Personality Traits**: Libras are known for their charming and diplomatic nature. They possess a strong sense of fairness. Their desire for harmony often leads them to seek compromise and avoid conflict.

COMPATIBILITY

Libras are most compatible with fellow Air signs like Gemini and Aquarius. They share similar intellectual and communicative qualities. They also tend to get along well with Fire signs, such as Aries, Leo and Sagittarius. These bring passion and energy to the relationship. However, their diplomatic nature means that Libras can also establish harmonious connections with individuals of various zodiac signs.

STRENGTHS

- **Charm and Grace:** Libras have an innate ability to put people at ease with their charm and social skills.
- **Diplomacy**: They excel at mediating conflicts and finding common ground in disputes.
- **Artistic Sensibility**: With Venus as their ruling planet, Libras often have a strong appreciation for art, beauty and aesthetics.

- **Fairness**: Libras have a strong sense of justice and fairness and are often advocates for equality.

WEAKNESSES

- **Indecisiveness**: Libras' desire for balance and harmony can sometimes lead to indecisiveness, as they weigh all options carefully.
- **Avoidance of Conflict**: They may avoid confrontations to maintain peace, even when addressing issues is necessary.
- **Dependency**: Libras may struggle with a tendency to seek validation and approval from others, which can lead to dependency.
- **Superficiality**: Their focus on aesthetics and surface harmony may sometimes make them appear superficial.

Welcome once again to our exploration of Libra! Symbolized by the scales representing balance, harmony and justice, Libra stands as the seventh sign in the zodiac. Governed by Venus and classified as an Air sign individuals with a Libra Sun are renowned for their charm, impartiality and artistic sensibilities. However, like all signs in astrology, they possess both strengths and weaknesses.

Subsequent chapters will take us on a journey into all aspects of Libras realm. We will unravel intricacies surrounding Libra's personality traits while delving into their perspectives on love and relationships. Furthermore we will uncover how their innate qualities influence their paths and personal development. Expect insights into compatibility, between Libra individuals and other zodiac signs while receiving guidance on embracing their strengths and overcoming challenges along the way.

Get ready to embark on an adventure of self exploration and growth! Whether you're a Libra searching for self awareness or simply curious about the world of astrology this guarantees to be an enriching and fulfilling exploration. Come along with us as we unravel the secrets of Libra and unlock its full power.

CHAPTER 1: HISTORY AND MYTHOLOGY

In this chapter we embark on an exploration of history and mythology. A journey to uncover the significance of the Libra star sign. Its roots extend far back into the fabric of civilization. As we delve into this chapter's pages we will journey back to ancient civilizations to explore some of the first observations and interpretations of Libra. From ancient stargazers to mythological tales we will discover how different cultures perceived and depicted Libra.

Our exploration doesn't end with history and astronomy alone. We will also meet Libra individuals who have shaped history and truly left a mark on our world. Furthermore we will examine the evolution of how Libra has been perceived and understood from ancient times up until today.

Now let us embark on a voyage through history and mythology influenced by the Libra zodiac sign. Together we will unveil the timeless wisdom and lasting impact of Libra!

HISTORICAL ORIGINS OF THE LIBRA CONSTELLATION

The constellation Libra, has a rich history dating back to ancient civilizations. Over the centuries, its symbolism has continued to evolve and influence culture. Here's a glimpse into some of its earliest history.

BABYLONIAN ASTRONOMY

The earliest known observations of Libra can be traced back to ancient Mesopotamia, particularly Babylon. The Babylonians recognized the stars within the constellation as early as 2000 BCE. They associated Libra with the concept of justice and balance. This was reflected in their legal and societal systems.

ANCIENT GREEK INFLUENCE

The Ancient Greeks adopted the Babylonian constellation system, incorporating Libra into their own celestial maps. However, in Greek mythology, Libra is often linked to the scales held by Astraea. She is the goddess of justice and is believed to have lived among humans during the Golden Age. She symbolizes the harmony and balance that humanity once enjoyed.

Themis, another Greek goddess of justice, is often associated with the scales. Her daughter, Dike, represents the concept of moral justice. The presence of these deities in Greek mythology underscores the idea of balance and fairness associated with Libra.

ROMAN INTERPRETATION

The Romans, influenced by Greek astronomy and mythology, adopted the concept of Libra as the Scales of Justice. The Roman association with this constellation further solidified its significance in matters of law and fairness.

CHINESE AND ARABIC VIEWS

In Chinese astronomy, the stars of Libra are often incorporated into other constellations, such as the adjacent Scorpius. Arabic astronomers, too, didn't have a distinct constellation corresponding to Libra. However they recognized the stars within it.

HINDU PERSPECTIVE

In Hindu astrology, the concept of Libra is not tied to a specific constellation. Instead it is represented through the zodiac sign of Tula. Tula is associated with balance and fairness. It is represented by a scale or a balance.

EGYPTIAN MYTHOLOGY

In Egyptian mythology the representation of Libra as we know it in contemporary astrology did not exist. However the core idea of balance and order which Libra represents in astrology held importance in their cosmology and religious beliefs.

Although there was no equivalent to the zodiac sign of Libra in Egypt the concept of balance and justice embodied by Libra found personification in the goddess Ma'at. Ma'at played a role in religion symbolizing truth, equilibrium order, harmony, lawfulness, morality and justice. Depictions often portrayed her with a feather adorning her hair. A feather that symbolizes truth itself.

HISTORICAL EVENTS UNDER THE LIBRA SEASON

Throughout history, many important events have occurred during the "Libra" season. Some astrologers believe these events may carry astrological significance. Here are some notable events which have occurred during the Libra season.

- **The Signing of the United Nations Charter** (June 26, 1945): The establishment of the United

Nations, an organization aimed at promoting peace and cooperation among nations, occurred during the Libra season. This event aligns with Libra's association with diplomacy and balance.
- **The Start of the French Revolution** (September 17, 1789): The French Revolution began during the Libra season. This was a period marked by calls for equality, justice and social harmony.
- **The Fall of the Berlin Wall** (November 9, 1989): The collapse of the Berlin Wall symbolized the reunification of East and West Germany. It occurred during the Scorpio-Libra cusp. This event represented a dramatic shift toward balance and reconciliation in a divided world.

HISTORICAL FIGURES BORN UNDER THE LIBRA SIGN

Several historical figures born under the Libra sign have made significant impacts on history.

- **Mahatma Gandhi** (October 2, 1869): Gandhi, born under the Libra sign, was a symbol of peace and nonviolent resistance. His leadership played a pivotal role in India's struggle for independence. He inspired movements for civil rights and freedom worldwide.
- **Eleanor Roosevelt** (October 11, 1884): As an American diplomat, humanitarian, and former First Lady, Eleanor Roosevelt advocated for civil rights, women's rights and social justice during her time. Her Libra traits of diplomacy and advocacy for fairness are evident in her legacy.

As we come to the end of this chapter we look back on the stories and historical significance associated with the Libra zodiac sign. From its early observations to modern astronomy, Libra has consistently represented values like balance, justice and harmony. The enduring legacy of Libra continues to have an impact today. Ultimately the teachings of Libra inspire all of us to seek equilibrium in our lives, fairness in our interactions and to appreciate beauty in life.

FURTHER READING AND REFERENCES

For readers eager to delve deeper into the history and mythology of Libra, as well as astrology in general, here is a list of primary sources, ancient texts and modern writings:

- **"Babylonian Star Catalogs"** - Explore ancient Babylonian records to uncover the earliest references to Libra in astronomy and astrology.
- **"The Works of Ptolemy"** - Ptolemy's "Tetrabiblos" is a classic text that delves into the principles of Western astrology.
- **"The Greek Myths"** by Robert Graves - This comprehensive work delves into Greek mythology, shedding light on the stories and deities associated with Libra's symbolism.
- **"Astrology: A Guide to Understanding Your Birth Chart" by Kevin Burk** - This modern guide offers a practical approach to understanding astrology, including insights into Libra's personality traits and influences.
- **"The Secret Language of Birthdays"** by Gary Goldschneider and Joost Elffers - This book provides detailed personality profiles for each day of the year, including those born under the Libra sign.
- **Online Resources**: Explore astrology websites, forums, and academic journals to keep up with the latest research and interpretations related to Libra and astrology in general.

CHAPTER 2:
LOVE & COMPATIBILITY

Few topics in the realm of astrology generate as much intrigue and curiosity as love and compatibility. In this chapter we embark on an exploration of how the Libra star sign approaches love and its compatibility with zodiac signs. We explore their qualities, desires and tendencies when it comes to love. From their pursuit of balance and partnership to their diplomatic disposition. In the following pages we uncover what makes Libra individuals such captivating companions in relationships.

However our exploration doesn't end with Libra. We will also examine how Libra's compatibility plays out with each of the twelve zodiac signs. If you're a Libra looking for insights into your love life or if you're fascinated by how astrology influences relationships this chapter will provide guidance.

THE LIBRA LOVE APPROACH

People born under the sign of Libra are seen as romantic and inclined towards building long term relationships. Let's take a closer look at how Libras approach love and romance.

- **Striving for Balance**; Libras are ruled by Venus, the planet of love and beauty. This greatly influences their perspective on romance. They aim to create equilibrium and harmony in all aspects of their lives including their relationships.
- **Focusing on Partnership**; Libras value the concept of partnership and companionship. They thrive when they are in a loving relationship. For them connection and shared experiences are musts. Being single for long periods does not typically satisfy a Libra. Ultimately they yearn to share their life with another.
- **Exuding Charm and Grace;** Libras are renowned for their charm, grace and impeccable manners. Overall this makes them especially appealing in matters of love. Furthermore they utilize their skills to create an inviting ambiance filled with romance.

- **Loyalty**; Once Libras are committed to a relationship they display unwavering loyalty and take their commitments seriously. They are willing to work through any challenges that arise to ensure harmony in their partnership. As such they expect their partners to reciprocate the same level of trust.
- **Conflict Avoidance**; Libras have an aversion to conflicts and confrontations. They prioritize maintaining peace and avoiding arguments within their relationships. While this trait can be considered positive it can also result in issues that require attention.
- **Appreciation for Aesthetics**; Libras possess an admiration for beauty and aesthetics. Art, music and the finer aspects of life hold beauty for them which they eagerly share with their partners.
- **Emphasis on Communication**; Effective communication holds importance for Libras when it comes to love. They value honest conversations with their partners as these conversations foster better harmony within the relationship. Libras excel at listening to others perspectives while empathizing with their loved ones emotions.

To sum it up when it comes to love and romance, Libras strive for equilibrium, charm and dedication. They have an inclination towards romantic gestures and place great importance on maintaining harmony in their relationships. While their desire for balance can be advantageous it is crucial for Libras to find ways to address conflicts in their pursuit of long lasting love.

COMPATIBILITY WITH OTHER ZODIAC SIGNS

LIBRA AND ARIES

Libra and Aries are both cardinal signs, which means they share a strong desire for leadership and action. While they have different approaches (Libra seeks balance, Aries seeks assertiveness), their dynamic can be invigorating and passionate. Libra can help Aries refine their impulsive nature. Aries can encourage Libra to be more decisive. With effort and understanding, this pairing can find a harmonious balance between Libra's diplomacy and Aries' enthusiasm.

LIBRA AND TAURUS

Libra and Taurus are both ruled by Venus. This connects them through a shared appreciation for beauty and sensuality. Taurus' stability and Libra's charm can create a secure and enjoyable partnership. Libra may introduce Taurus to more social experiences. Taurus can ground Libra in practicality. Their shared love of the finer things in life can make them compatible. However they may need to navigate Taurus' stubbornness and Libra's indecisiveness.

LIBRA AND GEMINI

Libra and Gemini are both air signs, fostering excellent communication and intellectual connection. They share a love for socializing, learning and exploration. This makes for a lively and engaging partnership. Libra's diplomacy can help ease Gemini's tendency to be indecisive. Gemini can stimulate Libra's curiosity. Their mental connection and shared interests often lead to a harmonious relationship.

LIBRA AND CANCER

Libra and Cancer have contrasting emotional needs and communication styles. Libra values harmony and intellectual connection. Cancer seeks emotional security and nurturing. Their differences may lead to misunderstandings. However, with effort, they can learn from each other. Libra can help Cancer express emotions more openly. Cancer can teach Libra the importance of emotional depth and security.

LIBRA AND LEO

Libra and Leo both appreciate socializing, beauty, and aesthetics, creating a vibrant and affectionate bond. Leo's warmth and generosity align well with Libra's charm and diplomacy. Both signs enjoy the finer things in life and can create an elegant and stylish partnership. Libra's willingness to compromise can help mitigate Leo's occasional need for attention.

LIBRA AND VIRGO

Libra and Virgo have significant differences in their approaches to life. Libra's focus is on balance. Virgo's is on details and practicality. Their connection may require effort. Libra may find Virgo too critical. Virgo may see Libra as indecisive. However, with patience and understanding, they can learn from each other. Overall they can create a complementary partnership.

LIBRA AND LIBRA

Two Libras share a strong intellectual connection and an appreciation for beauty and harmony. They value balance in their relationship and are skilled at resolving conflicts diplomatically. However, they may struggle with decision-making, as both tend to weigh options extensively. Overall, their shared values and social compatibility can create a harmonious partnership.

LIBRA AND SCORPIO

Libra and Scorpio are neighboring signs. They can either create a strong bond or lead to conflicts. Libra is diplomatic and seeks harmony. Scorpio is intense and desires depth in relationships. If they learn to appreciate each other's strengths and find a middle ground, their connection can be passionate and transformative. Trust and open communication are essential for this pairing to thrive.

LIBRA AND SAGITTARIUS

Libra and Sagittarius both enjoy socializing and exploring the world, creating a lively and adventurous partnership. They value freedom and independence. This they grant each other willingly. Libra's diplomacy can balance Sagittarius' bluntness. Sagittarius can inspire Libra to be more spontaneous. Their shared love for intellectual pursuits and optimism often leads to a harmonious and exciting relationship.

LIBRA AND CAPRICORN

Libra and Capricorn have differing approaches to life. Libra's focus is on relationships and aesthetics. This contrasts with Capricorn's practicality and ambition. While they may appear to be opposites, they can complement each other effectively. Libra can introduce Capricorn to the value of social connections and diplomacy. Capricorn can provide stability and security. With effort, they can create a partnership that combines beauty and practicality.

LIBRA AND AQUARIUS

Libra and Aquarius are both air signs, fostering excellent communication and intellectual connection. They share progressive and humanitarian values, creating a forward-thinking and innovative partnership. Both signs appreciate individuality and freedom, which they respect in each other. Their mental connection and shared ideals can often lead to a harmonious relationship.

LIBRA AND PISCES

Libra and Pisces have a natural affinity for each other, often forming a romantic and empathetic bond. Libra appreciates Pisces' sensitivity and creativity. Pisces admires Libra's charm and diplomacy. They share a love for art, beauty and romance. This leads to creating a dreamy and affectionate partnership. However, Libra's need for balance may clash with Pisces' occasional emotional turbulence, requiring understanding and patience to overcome.

TIPS FOR DATING AND MAINTAINING RELATIONSHIPS WITH LIBRA

DATING A LIBRA MAN

- **Engage in Intellectual Conversations**; Libra men enjoy stimulating discussions. Talk about topics like art, culture and current events to connect with them on a deeper level.
- **Set an Ambience**; Libra men have a soft side. Pay attention to creating a beautiful and unforgettable experience.
- **Respect Their Need for Personal Space**; While Libra men value relationships they also require some time and space. Allow them to pursue their

interests and maintain connections with their circles.
- **Be Patient with Decision Making;** Libra men can be indecisive as they carefully consider options. Practice patience. Avoid pressuring them when it comes to making choices whether decisions like dinner plans or more significant ones.

DATING A LIBRA WOMAN

- **Appreciate Their Social Nature**; Many Libra women are outgoing and enjoy socializing. Support their desire for a group of friends. Be open to attending social events together.
- **Compliment Their Sense of Style**; Libra women often have fashion sense. Compliment their style choices. Show appreciation for the effort they put into looking good.
- **Share Your Thoughts and Emotions**; Open communication is important to Libra women. Feel free to share your thoughts, emotions and any concerns you may have with them. This will help trust and a deeper understanding, between you both.
- **Balance**; Striving for balance is crucial when it comes to relationships with Libras. Aim for a partnership that's harmonious by being open to compromise and working together to find solutions that satisfy both of your needs.

Remember these tips can be helpful when dating or maintaining a relationship with a Libra individual.

However it's essential to recognize that everyone is unique. Building a long lasting connection requires understanding and appreciating each other's individuality and respecting each other's needs. Effective communication, trust and mutual respect form the foundation of any relationship.

As we wrap up our exploration of "Libra Love and Compatibility " we gain an understanding of how Libra's nature interacts with other zodiac signs. Throughout this journey we've discovered insights into how Libra approaches love and partnership. These insights serve as guidance for those navigating the tapestry of love and connection in their lives.

In conclusion we've learned that while astrology provides insights into relationship dynamics it is just one aspect of the complex dance known as love. Every person regardless of whether they're a Libra or have another zodiac sign brings their own uniqueness to any relationship. Ultimately the success of a relationship relies on communication, mutual respect and a shared commitment.

As you continue on your path may the wisdom and understanding gained from this chapter guide you towards embracing the beauty and equilibrium that Libra seeks in love. May it also help you build connections with those you encounter along the way. Love is a language that transcends signs. Ultimately it is within our power to shape heartwarming tales filled with beauty and serenity.

CHAPTER 3:
FRIENDS AND FAMILY

In the tapestry of connections few signs shine as brightly as Libra. In this chapter we embark on a journey into the realm of how Libra interacts with friends and family. Here we will be exploring the roles they assume and the dynamics they bring to these vital aspects of life.

Throughout this chapter's pages we will delve into the qualities that make Libra individuals such cherished friends and family members. However like any sign Libra also encounters challenges, within their friendships and familial relationships. These challenges will also be explored. As we delve into the realm of Libra's connections may you develop a better understanding of the roles they fulfill and the profound impact they have on the lives of those close to them.

LIBRA AS A FRIEND

Libra brings a delightful dynamic to friendship. With their ability to create harmony and balance in relationships Libras are often cherished companions. Here's a glimpse into what you can expect when you have a Libra as your friend.

- **Natural Mediators**; Libras act as peacemakers within their circles. They possess a talent for resolving conflicts and soothing tensions. If you find yourself in disagreement with someone, having a Libra friend by your side increases the likelihood of finding compromise and achieving resolutions.
- **Social**; Libras are like social butterflies. They effortlessly attract people with their charm and grace. As your friend they will introduce you to new people and make gatherings more enjoyable.
- **Engaging Conversationalists**; Libras genuinely care about others thoughts and emotions making them excellent conversationalists. They listen attentively to your ideas and feelings engaging you in discussions. Whether you need someone to bounce ideas off or simply share a chat with a Libra friend will be there for you.

- **Appreciation of Beauty**; Libras possess an admiration for art, culture and aesthetics. Expect them to introduce you to the wonders of beauty, in many forms. Whether it's through captivating art exhibitions or their impeccable fashion choices. They'll inspire you to see and embrace the beauty that surrounds us.
- **Dependable and Trustworthy**; Libras highly value trust in their relationships. As friends they are incredibly reliable and loyal. You can always rely on them to keep your secrets safe. They will stand by your side when you're in need of support.
- **Empathy**; Libras possess a strong sense of empathy and understanding. They genuinely strive to empathize with your perspective and offer advice. During times they will be there as a listening ear providing comfort with their words.
- **Love for Adventure**; Libras are always up for new experiences and exciting adventures. They'll be the ones to suggest road trips or weekend getaways. With a Libra friend you can anticipate a blend of planned activities along with escapades.
- **Fairness**; Fairness holds great importance for Libras when it comes to friendships. They make sure that your needs and opinions are respected and taken into consideration seriously. If any conflicts arise they approach them with grace while striving for a resolution.
- **Supportive and Encouraging**; When it comes to cheering others on Libras excel at being cheerleaders. They will wholeheartedly support your goals and aspirations providing you with encouragement and motivation every step of the

way. When you have a friend who's a Libra they empower you to chase after your dreams.

In essence having a Libra as a friend means being in the company of someone who deeply values friendship. They constantly strive for harmony and fairness bringing an air of elegance to your interactions. Having them as part of your circle of friends is truly delightful.

LIBRA AND FAMILY DYNAMICS

Within the interplay of family dynamics, the seventh sign of the zodiac, Libra brings forth a unique set of qualities and influences. Libras, renowned for their skills, charm and commitment to maintaining balance hold a key role in shaping familial dynamics. Let's delve deeper into how individuals with a Libra nature contribute to the tapestry of family life.

- **The Peacemaker**; Libras often find themselves assuming the role of peacemakers within their families. Their diplomatic approach and tact allow them to defuse tensions and resolve conflicts effectively. Whenever disagreements arise among family members you can count on a Libra to create an atmosphere of harmony.
- **Cultivating Family Bonds and Togetherness**; Family connections hold tremendous value for Libras. They consistently prioritize spending quality time with their loved ones. Initiating family gatherings, outings or special celebrations is something they actively engage in. Overall their

aim is to strengthen bonds while nurturing a sense of unity.

- **The Fair minded Parent**; When it comes to parenting roles, Libra parents strive for fairness and justice. Their mission is to ensure that every decision is equitable, by considering each child's needs.
- **The Creative and Homemaker**; Libras have an eye for beauty. Frequently they contribute to enhancing the family's living space making it visually welcoming. They enjoy decorating their homes, organizing family gatherings and creating a harmonious environment for their loved ones.
- **Striving for Equilibrium**; Libras bring a sense of balance to family dynamics encouraging compromise and fairness in decision making processes. They may act as the voice of reason during family discussions urging all members to express their viewpoints.
- **Conflict Avoidance**; Libras often go to great lengths to sidestep conflicts within the family unit in order to maintain harmony. While this trait can be advantageous it can also pose challenges when important matters are left unresolved. Remember it is crucial for Libras to strike a balance between preserving peace and addressing issues.
- **The Social Connectors**; Libras have a knack for introducing their family members to other people, expanding the network and connections within the family. They truly enjoy hosting get-togethers bringing together friends and family in an atmosphere of harmony.

In summary Libras play a role in shaping family dynamics by promoting fairness, balance and harmony. They excel in their abilities as peacemakers, diplomats and creators of a visually appealing family environment. While their inclination to avoid conflict can be advantageous it's important for Libras to address and resolve family matters to maintain a balanced dynamic within the family.

CHALLENGES IN FRIENDSHIPS AND FAMILY RELATIONS FOR LIBRA

While individuals born under the zodiac sign Libra possess qualities that contribute to their friendships and family relationships they also encounter specific hurdles. Being aware of these challenges can assist Libras in navigating their interactions effectively. Here are some common obstacles that Libras may come across.

- **Difficulty Making Decisions**; One of the challenges faced by Libras is their inclination, towards indecisiveness. They tend to weigh the pros and cons of choices which can result in frustration for friends and family.
- **Avoidance of Confrontation;** Libras possess an aversion to conflict. Often they will go to great lengths to evade it. While this may foster a tranquil atmosphere it can also lead to issues.
- **Trouble Saying "No"**; The desire to maintain harmony can make it arduous for Libras to say no. Consequently they may find themselves overcommitted and stressed out as they take on more than they can manage.
- **Seeking Validation from Others**; Libras frequently seek validation and approval from others. This makes them susceptible to peer pressure or the influence of people's opinions. Which can result in decisions that do not align with their desires.
- **Struggles, with Confrontation**; When it comes to facing confrontation or receiving criticism Libras often find it difficult to assert themselves. They tend to shy away from addressing issues. Overall it can hinder conflict resolution and impede personal growth.
- **Balancing Relationships**; One of the challenges that Libras encounter is finding a balance in their relationships. Especially when conflicts or tensions

arise. Ultimately they may feel torn between their loyalty to individuals.

- **Overemphasis on Aesthetics**; Libra's deep appreciation for beauty and aesthetics sometimes leads them to place importance on appearance. This can cause them to prioritize surface level aspects of relationships over fostering deeper connections.
- **Difficulty in Letting Go**; Libras have a tendency to hold onto relationships even when they have run their course hoping to restore harmony. Consequently they may struggle with letting go of friendships or family connections that're no longer healthy or beneficial.
- **Striving for Perfection**; Setting high standards for themselves and others is something Libras often do. This can result in disappointment when reality falls short of their expectations.

To overcome the obstacles they face and strengthen their relationships, individuals born under the zodiac sign of Libra can focus on developing assertiveness, making decisions and addressing conflicts in a manner. It is crucial for them to strike a balance between their desire for harmony and the need for communication. By engaging in these practices Libras have the opportunity to enhance and fortify their relationships.

In this chapter we have explored how Libras influence their friends and family members. Their ability to create harmony reflects their dedication to the well being of those they cherish. However we have also discussed some challenges that Libras may encounter, such as indecisiveness or avoidance of conflicts. It is important to note that despite these traits causing obstacles in relationships, Libras possess the capacity for growth and improvement. This enables them to navigate these challenges effectively.

By embracing their strengths facing challenges head on and consistently nurturing connections, with others Libras can cultivate relationships.

CHAPTER 4: CAREER AND MONEY

In this chapter we will delve into the workplace preferences, career goals, strengths and challenges that shape individuals born under the zodiac sign of Libra. Known for their ability to maintain balance and harmony, Libras often find themselves drawn towards roles that allow them to utilize their diplomatic skills. They have a talent for mediation. They are skilled negotiators who prioritize fairness in all their interactions. This quality makes them highly valued in professions where a strong sense of justice and the ability to see things from perspectives crucial.

Libras also possess a sense and a deep appreciation for beauty, which often leads them to excel in fields related to art, design and creative industries. Their keen eye for detail combined with their understanding of harmony makes them well suited for careers that require both creativity and practicality. In this chapter we will explore how these unique qualities influence their career choices and professional growth.

However just like every other sign has its challenges Libras are not exempted. We will also examine the difficulties they may encounter in the workplace. Their aversion to conflict and constant desire for consensus can sometimes result in indecisiveness or hesitancy to take a stance on matters. Understanding these challenges is crucial, in harnessing their potential.

Furthermore we will explore how Libras manage their finances. Libras are known for their balanced approach to decisions but they also have a penchant for luxury and aesthetics which can sometimes lead to indulgent spending. In this guide we will explore strategies that can help Libras maintain stability while satisfying their tastes.

So dear reader, get ready for a journey into the realm of career and finances from a Libras perspective. This chapter aims to provide an understanding and practical tips on how to harness the talents and inclinations of Libras in their professional lives.

CAREER PREFERENCES AND PROFESSIONAL ASPIRATIONS

Individuals born under the sign of Libra bring a unique set of qualities to the workplace. Here are some key aspects regarding Libras inclinations when it comes to careers.

- **Diplomats**; Libras excel in positions that necessitate mediation and diplomacy. They possess a talent for resolving conflicts. Naturally this makes them valuable team members and leaders in workplaces that prioritize collaboration and cooperation. Professions such as law, negotiation, counseling or human resources are well suited for their skill set.

- **Advocates for Justice;** Libras are inclined towards professions that involve advocating for fairness and justice. They are often motivated by the desire to make a positive impact on society. This can lead them towards careers in law, social work, advocacy or nonprofit organizations dedicated to social justice causes.
- **Creativity and Aesthetics**; Libras have an appreciation for beauty and aesthetics. This makes them well suited for careers in the arts or design fields such as fashion or interior decoration.
- **Social Butterflies;** Libras thrive in social situations. As such they are often attracted to careers, in fields like relations, marketing, event planning and customer service. Here their people skills and charisma can really shine.
- **Intellectual Pursuits;** Libras have a curiosity and a passion for challenges. They may be inclined towards careers in academia, research, journalism or any field that allows them to engage in thought provoking conversations and explore ideas.
- **Teamwork**; Libras excel as both leaders and team players. They strive to create a work environment that encourages open communication.
- **Entrepreneurship**; Some Libras are drawn to entrepreneurship as it allows them to utilize their creativity, diplomacy and sense of balance.

STRENGTHS IN THE WORKPLACE

Libra individuals bring a powerful set of strengths to the workplace making them highly valuable there. Their natural charm and diplomatic abilities, coupled with a commitment to balance and harmony contribute significantly to their success in professional settings. Here are the key strengths that distinguish Libra individuals.

- **Diplomacy**; Libras excel in resolving conflicts and finding common ground in disputes. Overall they contribute to fostering a productive atmosphere.
- **Charisma and Approachability**; Libra's charming and sociable nature makes them incredibly easy to work with. They effortlessly build relationships with colleagues creating a sense of camaraderie and cooperation.
- **Communication**; Libras are communicators who can express themselves clearly and persuasively

both in written form or when speaking. This valuable skill greatly enhances team collaboration efforts as well as interactions with clients.
- **Commitment to Fairness and Justice;** Libras have a strong sense of ethics and fairness. They passionately advocate for fair treatment of their colleagues making them reliable champions for equality and justice.
- **Team Player Mentality;** Libras thrive within team environments where they positively contribute to group dynamics by encouraging teamwork. They ensure that every voice is heard and foster collaboration within teams.
- **Expertise in Negotiation**; Libras possess excellent negotiation skills that enable them to navigate situations, with finesse. Whether they involve business deals, contracts or workplace conflicts is crucial for achieving successful outcomes.
- **Detail oriented**; Paying attention to the details in their work is a strength of Libras. This trait proves valuable in roles that demand precision, such as project management, quality control and design.
- **Aesthetic appreciation;** Libra's sense of style and appreciation for aesthetics can be advantageous in fields and industries where visual presentation holds importance. They possess an eye for design and can positively contribute to projects that require an element of beauty.
- **Flexibility**; Libras can handle changing circumstances and unexpected challenges with grace. Overall this makes them valuable assets in dynamic work environments.

- **Leaders**; When it comes to leadership potential Libras shine brightly. They prioritize fairness and teamwork while leading by example. Their leadership style fosters a work culture that inspires others to excel and collaborate.
- **Balanced perspective;** Libras approach problem solving with a balanced perspective by considering alternative viewpoints. Their ability to see the bigger picture and explore diverse solutions proves highly beneficial, in decision making processes.
- **Connector**; Building networks is something that Libras truly enjoy. They have a talent for forming connections. Furthermore they know how to use these relationships to advance their careers and benefit their organizations.

Overall Libras are highly committed to professional growth. They are always striving to improve themselves. Whether it's to seek out opportunities for learning and development or staying informed about the industry trends and best practices. In the workplace Libras excel as team players, effective communicators and advocates for fairness and harmony. Their unique strengths contribute to creating a productive work environment making them an invaluable asset to any organization.

CHALLENGES FACED BY LIBRA AND STRATEGIES TO OVERCOME THEM

While individuals born under the zodiac sign Libra possess a range of strengths that greatly contribute to their professional lives they also encounter challenges that may impede their career growth. By recognizing and addressing these challenges head on Libras can thrive in any workplace setting. Here are some common career hurdles faced by Libras and effective strategies to overcome them.

Difficulty in Decision Making

- Challenge; Libras often find it challenging to make decisions as they meticulously analyze all options.
- Strategy; To overcome this challenge Libras can set deadlines for decision making. Learn to trust their instincts. Seeking advice from trusted colleagues can provide insights and clarity.

Conflict Avoidance

- Challenge; Libras tend to shy away from conflicts. This can result in long term unresolved issues.
- Strategy; Developing assertiveness skills is crucial for Libras to address conflicts constructively. By learning how to diplomatically communicate concerns and resolving conflicts directly they can foster better relationships within the workplace.

External Validation Dependency

- Challenge; Libras commonly seek approval and validation from others. This leads to self doubt and excessive reliance on feedback.
- Strategy; It is important for Libras to build self confidence and prioritize self validation. Acknowledging achievements and placing trust in their judgment will reduce dependency on external opinions.

Overcommitment

- Challenge; Libras often fall into the trap of overcommitting themselves due to their desire for balance.
- Strategy; To avoid this challenge it's essential for Libras to prioritize tasks effectively by setting boundaries. Furthermore, learning when it's necessary to say no is key.

Burn out

- Challenge; Libras often find themselves overwhelmed and burdened by their desire to please others resulting in taking on responsibilities.
- Strategy; To avoid burnout Libras should prioritize their tasks. It's crucial for them to effectively manage their workload to maintain a work life balance.

Procrastination

- Challenge; Due to their inclination towards balance Libras may tend to procrastinate when faced with challenging tasks.
- Strategy; To overcome this challenge Libras can break down tasks into manageable steps and assign deadlines for each step. Creating a structured to do list can greatly assist in staying organized and motivated.

Self Criticism

- Challenge; Libra's tendency towards high standards often leads them down a path of self

criticism and perfectionism. This ultimately results in overload and stress.
- Strategy; To combat this challenge Libras need to cultivate self compassion and recognize their achievements even if they fall short of perfection. Setting goals and focusing on progress rather than striving for flawlessness can help alleviate this internal struggle.

Taking Initiative

- Challenge; Libras tend to wait for others to take charge in projects or decision making processes.
- Strategy; Libras can boost their confidence by seizing the initiative and actively seeking opportunities to lead or contribute their ideas. Ultimately stepping out of their comfort zone can facilitate growth.

Conflict Resolution Skills

- Challenge; While Libras prefer avoiding conflicts they may lack the skills needed to address them effectively when necessary.
- Strategy; Libras can invest in conflict resolution training. Develop assertiveness skills. Learning how to deal with conflicts and engage in conversations can enhance their professional relationships.

By acknowledging the obstacles they face and adopting strategies to overcome them Libras can utilize their strengths in the workplace while still upholding their commitment to maintaining harmony.

Throughout this chapter we have explored the qualities and characteristics that define Libras in their financial lives. With their charm, diplomacy and dedication to fairness and equilibrium Libras are well equipped to excel in fields.

When it comes to financial matters Libras strike a balance between their love for elegance and a practical approach to managing money. They appreciate the finer things in life. Also they understand the importance of responsible financial planning. This combination of valuing luxury while being financially prudent is evident in how they handle budgeting, investing and saving.

Whether you're a Libra seeking guidance on your career and financial journey or simply intrigued by the traits associated with this zodiac sign, let the insights from this chapter be your guiding light. Allow it to illuminate your path as you navigate through the realms of work and finance, with grace and equilibrium.

CHAPTER 5: SELF-IMPROVEMENT

In the adventure of life, the pursuit of personal growth is a universal theme that resonates with everyone. For those born under the sign of Libra, this journey takes on a fascinating dimension. In this chapter we delve into the art of self improvement through the lens of Libra's qualities and characteristics. We will see how they can navigate their personal growth journey by leveraging their strengths while addressing areas for improvement.

Whether you're a Libra looking for insights into your journey or someone fascinated by the traits of this zodiac sign this chapter guarantees to provide helpful guidance. Furthermore it will give you a deeper comprehension of how Libra approaches the timeless quest of self improvement.

PERSONAL GROWTH AND DEVELOPMENT

Personal growth is a journey that lasts a lifetime. For a Libra it presents an opportunity to refine their qualities, build upon their strengths and tackle their challenges. Here are some important areas where Libra individuals can experience growth and development.

- **Embracing Decisiveness**; Making decisions can be a challenge for Libras since they tend to consider all options. Remember that personal growth entails becoming more decisive. Practice making choices without overthinking. Trust your intuition.
- **Assertiveness Training**; To overcome their inclination to avoid conflict and seek validation Libras can focus on developing assertiveness skills. Learning how to express their needs, opinions and boundaries is an asset.
- **Self Validation**; Building self confidence and self validation should be emphasized by Libras. They can remind themselves that their worth isn't solely dependent on the approval of others.
- **Establishing Boundaries**; Personal growth involves setting boundaries in relationships and commitments. Learning to say "no" when

necessary while prioritizing self care contributes to a fulfilling life.

- **Overcoming Perfectionism**; Libras should strive to overcome their inclination towards perfectionism. It's important for them to embrace progress, rather than obsessing over flawlessness. By setting goals and celebrating their achievements even if they're not flawless Libras can foster growth.
- **Communication**; Personal development for Libras involves refining their communication skills. They can work on expressing themselves, handling conflicts constructively and actively listening to others.
- **Taking Initiative**; Libras should challenge themselves by stepping out of their comfort zones and taking initiative in their lives. This may involve seeking leadership roles pursuing opportunities or actively participating in decision making processes.
- **Conflict Resolution Skills**; Developing conflict resolution skills is vital for growth among Libras. They can learn to approach conflicts with an open mind seeking beneficial solutions and addressing issues promptly and constructively.
- **Embracing Self Care**; Prioritizing self care is crucial for the growth of Libra individuals. By establishing routines that nurture their emotional and mental well being they can maintain a sense of harmony in their lives.
- **Exploring Individuality**; Alongside enjoying interactions Libras can foster growth by exploring their own uniqueness and interests. It's important for them to dedicate time to cultivate their

hobbies, passions and talents while maintaining a rounded social life.
- **Goal Setting**; Setting attainable goals plays a role in personal growth, for everyone, including Libras. Libra individuals have the ability to create a roadmap, for their professional goals, which helps them maintain focus and motivation.

By embracing these areas of growth Libras can enhance their well being, relationships and career success. By doing so they can stay true to their commitment to balance and harmony, in all aspects of life.

HARNESSING LIBRA STRENGTHS AND OVERCOMING WEAKNESSES

Libra individuals have a set of strengths and weaknesses. Just like anyone else with a zodiac sign. Thus it's important for them to understand how to utilize their strengths while also addressing their areas for improvement. Ultimately it will help them to grow personally and achieve success. Here are some ways Libras can do that.

HARNESSING STRENGTHS

- **Diplomacy and Mediation**; Libras excel at resolving conflicts and facilitating harmonious communication. This makes them exceptional at mediating disputes in professional settings. Overall they have the ability to promote harmony and understanding.

- **Communication Skills**; Libras possess communication skills that can be utilized in leadership roles, public speaking engagements and effective collaboration within teams. Their ability to express ideas often inspires others.
- **Fairness and Justice**; Libra's commitment to fairness can drive them to advocate for fair causes. Volunteer work or actively participate in organizations focused on promoting equality and justice.
- **Charm and Likeability**; Libras charm and likability make them natural networkers who can build connections that help advance their careers.
- **Creativity and Aesthetics**; Libra's appreciation for aesthetics can be channeled into careers within design, art or other creative fields. Here their keen eye for detail and style leads to innovative and visually appealing work.

OVERCOMING WEAKNESSES

- **Dealing with Indecisiveness**; To tackle indecisiveness Libras can set concrete deadlines for making decisions. Trust their instincts. Seeking advice from trusted individuals can also help them feel more confident in their choices.
- **Addressing Conflict Avoidance**; Libras can overcome their tendency to avoid conflict by learning diplomatic ways to resolve conflicts. It's important for them to directly and assertively address issues with clear communication.
- **Reducing Dependency on External Validation;** To become less reliant on external validation Libras should focus on building self acceptance. Recognizing their worth and acknowledging their achievements is crucial.
- **Managing Overcommitment**; Libras can handle overcommitment by setting boundaries and learning to say "no" when necessary. Prioritizing self care and striving for balance is vital in order to avoid burnout.
- **Overcoming Procrastination;** To combat procrastination Libras can break tasks into small steps. Furthermore they can set deadlines for themselves and establish structured routines. It's important for them to focus on progress rather than seeking perfection.
- **Balancing Multiple Relationships;** For managing many relationships Libras can organize their commitments carefully, maintain open communication with loved ones and prioritize their own well being.

- **Overcoming perfectionism;** Libras can combat their perfectionism tendencies by setting goals and acknowledging their accomplishments even if they aren't flawless. Embracing progress, then striving for perfection is crucial.

For Libra individuals the process of harnessing their strengths and addressing their weaknesses is continuous. By focusing on growth they can lead balanced and fulfilling lives.

In this chapter we have deeply explored the art of self improvement guided by the principles that Libras hold dear; balance, harmony and fairness. We have discovered how Libras wholeheartedly embrace the journey of self improvement, with a sense of equilibrium and justice.

Libras understand that personal growth is a process that requires self awareness and a commitment to better oneself. They recognize the value of nurturing their strengths while addressing their weaknesses striving for a character. This journey exemplifies the power of self awareness and personal growth as Libras continuously evolve themselves. They seek harmony not only within themselves but in all aspects of life from personal relationships to professional pursuits.

As Libras embark on this path of self improvement they demonstrate how maintaining balance in one's character and actions can lead to development. Their dedication to finding equilibrium in emotions, thoughts and behaviors serves as an inspiration for others. Their journey motivates those around them to also strive for balance and harmony in their lives.

To summarize, this chapter not only showcases the qualities of Libras in their pursuit of self improvement but also emphasizes the broader impact of their journey. It is a journey that resonates with themes like growth, balance and the unwavering pursuit of becoming oneself. All while embracing life's challenges and opportunities, with a harmonious and balanced approach.

CHAPTER 6:
THE YEAR AHEAD

Dear Libra, we are delighted to invite you to a chapter that focuses on exploring the influences that will shape your life in the year ahead. As the stars gracefully move and align in their dance they offer insights into various aspects of your life. This celestial journey will shed light on areas, including love and relationships, career aspirations, financial stability, health and more.

Our goal, as we embark on this voyage together is to provide you with an understanding of how these celestial bodies may impact your experiences. Whether its Venus gently influencing your encounters or Mars fueling ambition within your pursuits or even the introspective effect of Mercury during retrograde periods – each astrological event carries significance.

That's not all. This chapter goes beyond predictions; it serves as a tool to help you harness the energies of the universe in your favor. We will navigate through times predicted by the stars while offering insights into making the most of moments and gracefully maneuvering through difficult periods with resilience.

Libra let us embark together on this captivating journey, with minds and hopeful hearts. As we move forward in the year, allow the stars to serve as beacons lighting your way and helping you synchronize your actions with the flow of life. Embrace this journey through the year filled with opportunities for growth and exciting discoveries.

HOROSCOPE GUIDE

As a Libra, you are known for your diplomacy, charm and commitment to harmony. Remember that you possess the qualities needed to navigate any challenges and embrace opportunities with grace. Trust in your innate ability to find equilibrium and harmony in all aspects of life. May the stars guide you on your journey, Libra, as you continue to shine with your unique blend of charm, diplomacy and elegance.

- **Aries (March 21 - April 19);** This year, Aries individuals may enter your life. They will be bringing a dynamic energy that can inspire your own pursuits. Embrace their adventurous spirit and consider taking calculated risks in your career or personal life.
- **Taurus (April 20 - May 20);** Taurus energies encourage you to focus on financial stability and personal values. This is an excellent time to reassess your budget. Make wise investments and prioritize your long-term financial goals.
- **Gemini (May 21 - June 20);** Gemini influences may spark your curiosity and desire for intellectual growth. Engage in learning opportunities. Take short trips. Foster open communication in your relationships.
- **Cancer (June 21 - July 22);** Cancer energies inspire emotional depth and connection in your

relationships. Focus on nurturing your closest bonds. Both romantic and familial. Remember to also strengthen your emotional well-being.
- **Leo (July 23 - August 22);** Leo influences may encourage you to shine in your career and take on leadership roles. Embrace your natural charisma and seize opportunities for professional growth.
- **Virgo (August 23 - September 22);** Virgo energies encourage you to pay attention to your health and well-being. Prioritize self-care routines, dietary habits. Exercise to maintain balance and vitality.
- **Libra (September 23 - October 22);** This year, focus on your personal growth journey. Embrace your diplomatic nature to resolve any conflicts in your life. Harness your charm to build positive relationships.
- **Scorpio (October 23 - November 21);** Scorpio influences may bring transformative experiences. Embrace change, let go of what no longer serves you. Trust in your ability to rise from any challenges.
- **Sagittarius (November 22 - December 21);** Sagittarius energies inspire adventure and exploration. Plan a trip or embark on a new educational journey to broaden your horizons.
- **Capricorn (December 22 - January 19);** Capricorn influences encourage you to focus on your finances. Set clear financial goals, manage your resources wisely. Invest in long-term stability.
- **Aquarius (January 20 - February 18);** Aquarius energies may bring new friendships and opportunities for collaboration. Embrace your

social side and join group activities. Contribute to causes that matter to you.

- **Pisces (February 19 - March 20);** Pisces influences inspire your spiritual growth. Explore mindfulness practices, meditation, or yoga to connect with your inner self. Strive to find peace and balance.

KEY ASTROLOGICAL EVENTS AND THEIR IMPACT ON LIBRA

Astrological events can have a significant influence on Libra individuals, guiding their experiences and personal growth throughout the year. Here are some key astrological events and their potential impact on Libra.

- **New Moon in Libra (Date Varies Each Year);** The New Moon in Libra marks a powerful time for self-reflection and setting intentions. Libras can use this period to focus on personal goals. Especially those related to balance, harmony and relationships.
- **Mercury Retrograde (Multiple Times a Year);** Mercury Retrograde periods may bring communication challenges and misunderstandings. Libras should be cautious in their interactions and use these times for reflection. Work on resolving any lingering issues in their relationships.
- **Venus Retrograde (Happens Approximately Every 18 Months);** Venus, Libra's ruling planet, occasionally goes into retrograde. During this time, Libras may reevaluate their values and

relationships. Ultimately it's a period for introspection and possibly making changes in these areas.

- **Full Moon in Libra (Date Varies Each Year);** The Full Moon in Libra illuminates the need for balance and fairness in your life. It may bring clarity to your relationships and help you make decisions regarding partnerships and commitments.
- **Jupiter in Air Signs (Approximately Every 12 Years);** When Jupiter, the planet of expansion and growth, transits through air signs like Gemini or Aquarius, it can bring opportunities for intellectual growth, travel. It's about expanding our horizons. Libras may find themselves drawn to higher education, travel adventures, or broadening their knowledge during these periods.
- **Saturn in Air Signs (Approximately Every 28-29 Years);** Saturn's transit through air signs can lead to significant life changes and personal growth. It may challenge Libras to redefine their goals and ambitions. This can lead to fostering a more structured and disciplined approach to their lives.
- **Lunar and Solar Eclipses (Multiple Times a Year);** Eclipses often signify endings and beginnings. Libras should pay attention to eclipses in their birth chart. They can herald shifts in relationships, career, or personal identity. These times may prompt transformative experiences.
- **Venus in Libra (Periodic Transit);** When Venus, your ruling planet, transits through Libra, it enhances your natural charm and appeal. It's a

favorable time for love, romance and enhancing your personal style.

- **Mars Retrograde (Happens Approximately Every 2 Years)**; Mars Retrograde can bring a slowdown in energy and motivation. Libras may need to be patient and avoid impulsive actions during this time. Reassess and refine your goals and actions.
- **Sun Entering Libra (Around September 23);** As the Sun enters Libra, it marks the start of Libra season. This is a time when your strengths and qualities shine brightly. It's an excellent period for setting intentions and strengthening relationships.

The above astrological events can serve as guides for Libra individuals. Knowledge of them will help to navigate life's twists and turns while staying true to their commitment to harmony and fairness. Embrace these celestial influences and use them as opportunities for personal growth throughout the year.

KEY LIFE AREAS

The year ahead promises a journey of self-discovery, personal growth and transformation for Libra individuals. By navigating the celestial influences wisely and with intention, you can enhance your life in many ways. Now let's take a look at some key areas.

LOVE AND RELATIONSHIPS

The year ahead brings a transformative wave in the romantic life of Libra individuals. Venus, your ruling planet, embarks on a journey that amplifies your charm and enhances your relationships.

Key Periods:

- February to April: A time of renewed passion and deeper connections. Venus aligns with Jupiter. Now is a chance for new love or the rekindling of old flames.
- Mid-July: A potential period of turbulence. Mars's influence may bring challenges that test the strength of your relationships.
- Advice: Embrace honesty and open communication. This year is an excellent opportunity to build stronger, more meaningful bonds.

CAREER AND FINANCES

Jupiter's transit through your career house heralds a period of expansion and growth in your professional life. However, be wary of Saturn's retrograde phase. It may bring about unexpected challenges.

Key Periods:

- Late March to June: Career growth is accelerated. Opportunities for promotion or new ventures are likely.
- September to November: Caution advised in financial matters. Saturn's influence may lead to delays or setbacks.
- Advice: Stay adaptable and open to new opportunities. Careful financial planning is essential during the latter half of the year.

HEALTH AND WELLNESS

Neptune's presence in your health sector suggests a need for balance in physical and mental wellness. It's a year to focus on holistic health.

Key Periods:

- April to May: Ideal for starting new health regimes or diets.
- August: Potential for stress-related issues. Prioritize mental health and relaxation.
- Advice: Regular exercise, balanced nutrition and mindfulness practices will be crucial in maintaining your health throughout the year.

PERSONAL GROWTH AND SELF-DISCOVERY

The year's planetary alignment encourages introspection and self-improvement for Libra individuals. Pluto's transformative energy is particularly influential, fostering deep personal changes.

Key Periods:

- January to March: Reflection and setting personal goals.
- October to December: A powerful period for self-discovery and implementing life changes.
- Advice: Utilize this year for self-reflection. Engage in activities that nurture your soul and help you connect with your true self. Be open to change and personal evolution.

Throughout this chapter we have discussed the significance of events in various aspects of life. These celestial happenings act as guiding stars that provide insights and opportunities to align yourself with your path. Always remember that you possess qualities like diplomacy, charm and an unwavering commitment to maintaining balance and harmony. With these traits combined with the guidance from the cosmos you are empowered to navigate both challenges and triumphs that lie ahead.

As you move forward into this year, embrace each astrological event as an opportunity for self discovery, progress and renewal. Seize these chances with grace and intention. May the upcoming year provide you with a canvas to create a beautiful and balanced masterpiece of your life.

CHAPTER 7:
FAMOUS LIBRA PERSONALITIES

In the celestial tapestry of the zodiac, Libra emerges as a constellation marked by its charm, diplomacy and commitment to balance. As we delve into this chapter, we embark on a captivating exploration of the lives and achievements of famous Libra individuals who have left an indelible mark on the world.

Libras are known for their elegance, artistic inclinations and the ability to bring equilibrium to any situation. They possess an innate sense of justice and a desire to foster peaceful coexistence. It is no wonder that many of history's most influential figures have been born under the Libra sign.

Within these pages, you will encounter an array of remarkable Libra personalities from diverse fields. Including politics, sports, music, film and more. Each of them embodies the unique qualities of Libra in their own exceptional way, leaving an enduring legacy for generations to come.

Join us as we celebrate the enchanting charm and profound impact of these famous Libra individuals. Through their stories and contributions, we gain a deeper understanding of the celestial gifts bestowed upon this remarkable sign.

MAHATMA GANDHI

- Date of Birth: October 2, 1869.
- Brief Biography: Mahatma Gandhi was a renowned Indian leader who played a pivotal role in the country's struggle for independence from British rule. He is known for his philosophy of nonviolent resistance and civil disobedience.
- Libra Traits: As a Libra, Gandhi embodied qualities of diplomacy, fairness, and a strong sense of justice. His commitment to nonviolence and peace aligns with Libra's desire for harmony.

- Impact: Gandhi's leadership and nonviolent approach to resistance inspired movements for civil rights and freedom around the world. He is remembered as a symbol of peace and is often referred to as the "Father of the Nation" in India.
- Personal Life: Gandhi lived a simple and ascetic life, dedicated to his principles. He was married to Kasturba Gandhi and had four children.

SERENA WILLIAMS

- Date of Birth: September 26, 1981.
- Brief Biography: Serena Williams is one of the greatest tennis players of all time. She has won numerous Grand Slam titles and is known for her powerful and dynamic playing style.
- Libra Traits: Serena's determination, sense of balance on the court, and ability to maintain composure under pressure reflect Libra's qualities of grace, poise, and competitiveness.
- Impact: Serena Williams has left an indelible mark on the world of tennis. Her accomplishments and advocacy for gender equality have made her an iconic figure in sports.
- Personal Life: Serena is the sister of Venus Williams, also a tennis champion. She is married to Alexis Ohanian, with whom she has a daughter.

JOHN LENNON

- Date of Birth: October 9, 1940.
- Brief Biography: John Lennon was a legendary musician and member of the iconic band The Beatles. He was a prolific songwriter and advocate for peace.
- Libra Traits: Lennon's artistic creativity, desire for harmony in his music and commitment to peace resonate with Libra's artistic and diplomatic qualities.
- Impact: His music with The Beatles and as a solo artist has left an enduring legacy in the music industry. Lennon's activism and calls for peace

made him a symbol of hope during turbulent times.
- Personal Life: Lennon was married to Yoko Ono. They were known for their activism and artistic collaborations.

BRIGITTE BARDOT

- Date of Birth: September 28, 1934.
- Brief Biography: Brigitte Bardot is a French actress, singer and fashion model. She became an international sex symbol during the 1950s and 1960s.
- Libra Traits: Bardot's beauty, elegance and allure on screen epitomize Libra's sense of aesthetics and charm.
- Impact: She was a cultural icon and influenced fashion and film during her era. Bardot's career and style have left a lasting mark on the entertainment industry.
- Personal Life: Bardot was married multiple times and later became an animal rights activist.

EMINEM

- Date of Birth: October 17, 1972.
- Brief Biography: Eminem, born Marshall Mathers, is a highly influential American rapper, songwriter and record producer.
- Libra Traits: Eminem's lyrical talent, storytelling abilities and his pursuit of balance in his personal

life are in line with Libra's artistic and harmonious inclinations.
- Impact: He is one of the best-selling music artists globally and has received numerous awards for his contributions to hip-hop and music in general.
- Personal Life: Eminem has faced personal struggles and addiction but has also championed self-improvement and sobriety.

MARGARET THATCHER

- Date of Birth: October 13, 1925.
- Brief Biography: Margaret Thatcher, also known as the "Iron Lady," was the first female Prime Minister of the United Kingdom. She held office from 1979 to 1990.
- Libra Traits: Thatcher's strong leadership, diplomacy in international relations, and her determination to restore economic balance in the UK resonate with Libra's qualities.
- Impact: She was a polarizing figure but left an indelible mark on British politics. Her conservative policies and strong leadership style defined an era.
- Personal Life: Thatcher was married to Denis Thatcher and had two children.

DWIGHT D. EISENHOWER

- Date of Birth: October 14, 1890.
- Brief Biography: Dwight D. Eisenhower, often called "Ike," was a five-star general during World

War II and the 34th President of the United States, serving from 1953 to 1961.
- Libra Traits: Eisenhower's diplomatic skills, sense of justice, and efforts to maintain international peace align with Libra's characteristics.
- Impact: As a military leader, he played a crucial role in the Allied victory in WWII. His presidency marked a period of relative stability in the United States during the 1950s.
- Personal Life: Eisenhower was married to Mamie Eisenhower. Together they had two children.

ELISABETH SHUE

- Date of Birth: October 6, 1963.
- Brief Biography: Elisabeth Shue is an American actress known for her roles in films like "The Karate Kid," "Back to the Future Part II," and "Leaving Las Vegas."
- Libra Traits: Shue's talent in the arts, her graceful presence on screen, and her ability to strike a balance in her diverse roles resonate with Libra's artistic and harmonious qualities.
- Impact: She has had a successful career in Hollywood and received critical acclaim for her performances, including an Academy Award nomination for "Leaving Las Vegas."
- Personal Life: Shue is married to film director Davis Guggenheim. Together they have three children.

CARDI B

- Date of Birth: October 11, 1992.
- Brief Biography: Cardi B, born Belcalis Marlenis Almánzar, is a Grammy-winning rapper, songwriter and actress. She is known for her chart-topping hits and outspoken personality.
- Libra Traits: Cardi B's artistic expression, charm, and ability to balance her career with her personal life align with Libra's creative and harmonious qualities.
- Impact: She has become a prominent figure in the music industry and a voice for female empowerment. Her music and outspoken nature have garnered a massive following.
- Personal Life: Cardi B is married to rapper Offset. Together they have a daughter.

VLADIMIR PUTIN

- Date of Birth: October 7, 1952.

- Brief Biography: Vladimir Putin is a Russian politician who served as the President of Russia and the Prime Minister at different times. He has been a prominent figure in Russian politics since the late 1990s.
- Libra Traits: Putin's diplomatic and strategic approach to international relations, as well as his ability to maintain balance in Russian politics, align with Libra's qualities.
- Impact: He has been a central figure in Russian politics, overseeing significant changes in the country's political landscape and international relations.
- Personal Life: Putin has kept his personal life relatively private. He was married to Lyudmila Shkrebneva and has two daughters.

ALFRED NOBEL

- Date of Birth: October 21, 1833.
- Brief Biography: Alfred Nobel was a Swedish chemist, engineer, and inventor known for inventing dynamite. He is also the founder of the Nobel Prizes, awarded for significant contributions to humanity.
- Libra Traits: Nobel's innovative spirit, his commitment to promoting peace and progress, and his desire to balance the destructive potential of explosives resonate with Libra's qualities.
- Impact: His invention of dynamite revolutionized construction and mining but also led to his concern about its potential misuse. He left his fortune to establish the Nobel Prizes. This

recognizes outstanding achievements in various fields.
- Personal Life: Nobel never married and had no children.

BARBARA WALTERS

- Date of Birth: September 25, 1929.
- Brief Biography: Barbara Walters is an American television journalist, known for her pioneering work in broadcast journalism and her interviews with prominent figures.
- Libra Traits: Walters' ability to mediate interviews, her sense of diplomacy in her reporting, and her knack for striking a balance between hard news and human interest stories align with Libra's qualities.
- Impact: She broke barriers for women in journalism and became one of the most respected figures in the industry. Her interviews with world leaders and celebrities have been iconic.
- Personal Life: Walters has been married four times and has one daughter.

As we conclude this chapter dedicated to the personalities of Libra we have embarked on a journey exploring the lives and achievements of these individuals who have graced our world with their unique talents.

From Mahatma Gandhi's philosophies to Serena Williams dynamic athleticism from Brigitte Bardot's captivating performances to Eminem's brilliance. Each of these individuals showcases their own distinctive interpretation of what it means to be a Libra. They have left a mark on the tapestry of history shaping realms such as politics, sports, music, film and beyond.

As we reflect on the contributions of Libra individuals let us keep in mind the qualities associated with this zodiac sign. Charisma, fairness and a strong sense of justice. Like these known personalities have gracefully and profoundly impacted the world stage, every Libra has the potential to utilize their celestial gifts. With those gifts they also can make a positive impact.

CONCLUSION

Finally we have arrived at the culmination of our journey exploring the fascinating realm of the Libra zodiac sign. It has been a voyage filled with exploration, enlightenment and a deeper understanding of individuals born under Libra. Now as we prepare to say goodbye to the balancing scales of Libra let's take a moment to ponder on the insights and revelations we have discovered. From delving into the historical origins and mythologies surrounding Libra to unraveling the intricacies of love, family connections and friendships. In the lives of those influenced by this sign we have embarked on an extensive expedition through a diverse landscape of knowledge and understanding. Here is a summary of the chapters we have traversed.

- **Chapter 1: History and Mythology** - In this chapter, we delved into the earliest observations of the Libra constellation in ancient civilizations. We explored how different cultures perceived and represented Libra in their star maps. We also uncovered the intriguing role of Libra in ancient mythologies, connecting the celestial scales to captivating tales of balance and justice.
- **Chapter 2: Love & Compatibility** - Here, we ventured into the realms of love and relationships. There we explored the personality traits, strengths, weaknesses and compatibility of Libra individuals with other zodiac signs. We unveiled the unique

approach Libras bring to love and romance, shedding light on their quest for balance and harmony.

- **Chapter 3: Friends And Family** - This chapter delved into the dynamics of Libra individuals in their friendships and family relationships. Here we highlighted their charming and diplomatic qualities. We also examined the challenges that Libras may face in maintaining these essential connections.
- **Chapter 4: Career And Money** - In the world of career and finances, we explored the preferences, strengths and potential challenges faced by Libra individuals. We uncovered their abilities to excel in the workplace. From there we offered insights into their diplomatic and balanced approach to professional aspirations.
- **Chapter 5: Self-Improvement** - This chapter guided us through the journey of personal growth and self-improvement for Libra individuals. We explored how Libras can harness their strengths and overcome weaknesses, fostering a deeper sense of self-awareness and development.
- **Chapter 6: The Year Ahead** - Here, we examined how astrological events impact the lives of Libra individuals in various aspects, including love, career, health and personal growth. We offered insights into the opportunities and challenges that may arise in the year ahead.
- **Chapter 7: Famous "Libra" Personalities** - Finally, we celebrated the extraordinary accomplishments and enduring legacies of famous Libra personalities who have left an indelible mark

on the world. From Mahatma Gandhi to Serena Williams, these individuals exemplify the grace, charm and impactful nature of Libra.

As we near the conclusion of our journey let us bid farewell to Libra. A sign that brings harmony and elegance to the universe. May the knowledge and wisdom acquired from our exploration of the Libra zodiac sign continue to light up your path and inspire you on your adventure.

As we draw near to wrapping up our journey our intention has been to celebrate and encourage Libra individuals to embrace their qualities and provide valuable insights for their future paths. Our exploration of what lies ahead for Libra has equipped readers with valuable knowledge while featuring profiles of notable personalities born under this zodiac sign that illustrate real life examples of its impact.

The important lesson from this book is to appreciate and celebrate the unique qualities of Libras. Libras you are known for being diplomatic, seeking balance and promoting harmony. Embrace your charm, artistic sensibilities and commitment to justice. The scales of Libra represent more than a symbol. They signify the gift you bring to the world. Embrace them as they hold the key to establishing connections, personal growth and creating a harmonious world.

To all those born under the Libra sign remember that you possess an ability for balance like no other. Utilize it to create beauty, foster understanding and bring harmony not into your life but also into the lives of those around you. Your natural charm, diplomacy skills and artistic sensibilities are your superpowers. Allow them to shine brightly.

As we conclude this book we encourage you to embrace the wisdom of Libra. Embody your qualities and seek balance in all aspects of life. Finally, allow the celestial bodies to serve as your guiding light on the path towards becoming the best version of yourself. In the tapestry of the Zodiac, you as a Libra shine brightly with beauty and harmony.

Subscribe To Sofia Visconti

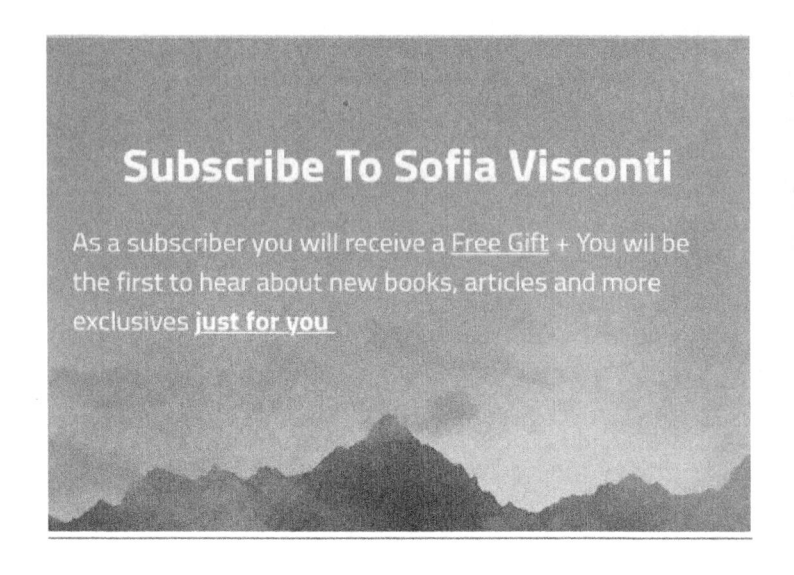

As a subscriber you will receive a _Free Gift_ + You wil be the first to hear about new books, articles and more exclusives **just for you**

Click Here

Or Visit Below:
https://www.subscribepage.com/svmyth

Or Simply Scan The Qr Code To Join

Printed in Great Britain
by Amazon